Ten-Minute Editing Skill Builders

by Murray Suid
illustrated by Philip Chalk

This book is for
Leslie Kallen

Publisher: Roberta Suid
Editor: Carol Whiteley
Design and Production: Philip Chalk

Other Monday Morning publications by the author:
*Book Factory, For the Love of Research, How to Be an Inventor,
How to Be President of the U.S.A., Picture Book Factory, Report Factory,
Storybooks Teach Writing, Ten-Minute Grammer Grabbers,
Ten-Minute Real World Writing Warm-ups, Ten-Minute Thinking Tie-ins,
Ten-Minute Whole Language Warm-ups*

For a complete catalog, write to the address above.
e-mail address: MMBooks@aol.com

Monday Morning is a registered trademark of
Monday Morning Books, Inc.

ISBN 1-878279-98-X

Printed in the United States of America
9 8 7 6 5 4 3 2 1

CONTENTS

INTRODUCTION

Editing (some people prefer the term "revising") is the key to good writing. Many authors say that rewriting is their favorite part of writing.

Unfortunately, students aren't born knowing how to polish stories, reports, letters, and other assignments. Fortunately, they can master this vital skill via quick, chalkboard practices.

Prescription for Editing Success

Just as a medical doctor pays attention to a variety of phenomena—blood pressure, reflexes, temperature, and so on—an editor must examine a piece of writing from many perspectives. These include:

- word choice
- organization
- facts
- spelling
- logic
- punctuation

Asking students to master these editing issues all at once can be overwhelming. A better strategy is to introduce them one at a time using short, error-filled practice sentences, which students deal with on a daily basis.

The Daily Edit

Ten-Minute Editing Skill Builders contains hundreds of editing examples representing common writing problems. You'll find a short, annotated lesson that suggests how to introduce each topic. You can then use the following four-step routine for reinforcing the skill with additional practices:

Step. 1. On the board or on an overhead projector, write an example for students to edit.

Step. 2. Give students a few minutes to read the example and then write an edited version in their notebooks. (There's no need for students to copy the error-filled example.)

Step 3. If time permits, have students go over their edited versions with a partner.

Step 4. Edit the example on the board to make sure that students understand the problem and the revision. If necessary, students should correct what they wrote in their notebooks.

Introduction

While each introductory example contains just one error, the reinforcement examples, appearing on the odd-numbered pages, may include two or more errors—one related to the main topic, and the others chosen randomly. These secondary errors add realism to the chalkboard editing. However, you can always omit the extra errors if you prefer a narrower editing focus.

There are many ways to adapt this method to your classroom. For example, after students gain experience, they can serve as "guest editors" in carrying out step 4. They might even create their own editing examples.

For a dramatized view of the Daily Edit routine, see the picture story on pages 6 and 7.

Beyond Ten Minutes

In addition to the chalkboard practices, you'll find an extension activity for each topic. For example, the dictionary hunt (page 8) reinforces the idea that proper nouns must be capitalized.

The Resources section at the back of the book contains a reproducible Editing Guide, which students can consult while doing the chalkboard edits or while working on their own papers.

Other resources are: a page of editing symbols, lists of tricky words you can use to make the chalkboard examples more challenging, and homonym riddles that provide fun spelling and vocabulary practice. You'll also find a model for teaching peer editing using editing notes.

Where to Begin

Editors must deal with whatever problems appear in a manuscript. One time the focus might be organization. Another time it could be wording or punctuation.

Because there is no one "right place" to begin, this book is organized alphabetically. You might start at the beginning, or you might prefer to zero in on problems that occur regularly in your students' writing.

Either way, skip around. Do a homonym spelling problem one day, and a trite-title exercise the next. Presenting random practices better prepares students for the unpredictable challenges of real-world writing.

The daily edit is a quick practice that builds the habit of revising while teaching spelling, punctuation, word choice, and other skills. The activity works like this.

The teacher or a student presents a sentence on the board or on an overhead projector. The passage usually contains one or a few errors.

A small whole can sink big Ship

Students read the passage and mentally edit it.

A small hole ~~whole~~ can sink a big Ship.

Some teachers encourage students to work together on the daily edit.

I think "whole" should be "hole."

Right. The two words are homonyms. "Whole" means all of something.

Each student writes the revised version on paper or in a notebook dedicated to the daily edit.

DAILY EDIT NOTEBOOK

The teacher now edits the text or asks students to suggest changes and give a reason for each revision.

ole g Ship.

The word "ship" shouldn't be capitalized because it's a common noun.

Introduction

Before asking students to handle a new kind of editing problem, introduce the concept.

We lost the game it was close, though.

Now, the problem with run-on sentences is...

In some cases, you might post rules students can refer to. While eventually students should know the rules by heart, the first goal is to encourage the habit of improving a text.

Comma Rules
1. Use commas to separate listed nouns.
2. Use a comma to separate clauses.

Another option is to give students an *Editing Guide*, such as the one found in the "Resources" section of this book.

"To change the passive voice to the active..."

You can even use games to give students the knowledge they'll need to be intelligent editors.

Period!—

To help ensure transfer of skills to actual writing, have students practice editing longer, error-filled texts.

Goldilocks and the 3 Bears

A final hint: On some days, present material with no errors. This will keep students on their toes and also teach them the important lesson that it's best to leave well enough alone.

To be or not to be, that is the question

CAPITALIZATION ERRORS

To prepare students for this exercise, you might first go over the rules in the Editing Guide, page 78.

DIRECTIONS:
1. On the board, write a sentence that contains several capitalization errors:

    last Summer, we visited mexico.

2. Ask students to edit the sentence.
3. Have students assist you as you edit the sentence:

    Last summer, we visited Mexico.

4. Discuss the reasons for each change:
   • Capitalize the first word in a sentence.
   • Do not capitalize the names of the four seasons.
   • Capitalize the names of countries because these are proper nouns.
5. Use the examples on the next page for more practice.

EXTENSION:
Send students on a dictionary hunt, looking for capitalized words or expressions. They should give a reason for each capitalized word that they find, for example:

    Cheyenne: Capitalize the names of nationalities.
    Chile: Capitalize the names of countries.

Editing Examples: Capitalization

First Draft	Edited Draft
1. more people speak chinese than any other language.	1. More people speak Chinese than any other language.
2. my favorite brand of cereal are crunchy pops.	2. My favorite brand of cereal is Crunchy Pops.
3. in july, 1969, neil armstrong became the 1st person to walk on the moon.	3. In July, 1969, Neil Armstrong became the first person to walk on the moon.
4. last Winter, we visited niagara falls our Hotel was in canada.	4. Last winter, we visited Niagara Falls. Our hotel was in Canada.
5. my youngest brothers favorite book is <u>where the wild things are</u>.	5. My youngest brother's favorite book is <u>Where the Wild Things Are</u>.
6. every 4 years, u.s. voters choose their president on the first tuesday after the first monday in november.	6. Every four years, U.S. voters choose their President on the first Tuesday after the first Monday in November. [Some experts capitalize the word "President," others don't.]
7. wilbur and orville wright of dayton, ohio, first flew their airplane on december 17, 1903, near kitty hawk, north carolina.	7. Wilbur and Orville Wright of Dayton, Ohio, first flew their airplane on December 17, 1903, near Kitty Hawk, North Carolina.
8. during the flood, the red cross gave supplies to many Families.	8. During the flood, the Red Cross gave supplies to many families.
9. seven countries make up central america: guatemala, el salvador, belize, honduras, nicaragua, costa rica, and panama.	9. Seven countries make up Central America: Guatemala, El Salvador, Belize, Honduras, Nicaragua, Costa Rica, and Panama.

CHOPPY WRITING

Although sentences that start with "And" aren't ungrammatical, long strings of them create an annoying, choppy style. Students need to be aware of the problem and how to overcome it.

DIRECTIONS:
1. On the board, write a passage that includes one or two sentences starting with "And," "But," or "So."

> **A big dog was chasing me. And it looked mean. And I couldn't find a place where to hide.**

2. Ask students to edit the sample.
3. Have students help you edit the sample:

> **A big, mean-looking dog was chasing me. I couldn't find a place to hide.**

4. Discuss the reasons for the changes:
   - Starting many sentences with "And" makes the writing seem repetitious.
   - Putting each fact in a separate sentence leads to a choppy and immature style.

Explain that the problem can be solved by combining sentences and deleting repetitious words.

5. Use the examples on the next page for more practice.

EXTENSION:
To help students overcome choppy writing, when assigning a paper limit the number of sentences that may start with "And," "But," "So," and "Then." Before you collect their papers, have students check for, and revise, problem sentences.

Editing Examples: Choppy Writing

First Draft	Edited Draft
1. I couldn't find anything worth watching on TV. So I turned off the TV.	1. Because I couldn't find anything worth watching on TV, I turned off the set.
2. I like to read mysteries. But I don't like to read animal stories. But I do enjoy adventure stories.	2. I like to read mysteries and adventure stories. On the other hand, I don't enjoy animal stories.
3. I was busy today. I cleaned my rom. And I swept the walk. And then I washed the dog.	3. I was busy today. First, I cleaned my room. Next, I swept the walk. Finally, I washed the dog. [Or: "I was busy today. I cleaned my room, swept the walk, and washed the dog."]
4. I kept a garden last summer. And it was hard work. And it was fun, too.	4. I kept a garden last summer. It was hard work, but fun.
5. I told my friend I wanted to see a movie. And my friend said he wanted to see one, too. And we discussed what to see. And then we couldn't agree. So we drew computer art instead.	5. My friend and I wanted to see a movie. We discussed which one, but we couldn't agree what to see. In the end, we drew computer art.
6. A family recently moved into my neighborhood. They came from India. They plan to stay here for a year. And they might stay longer.	6. A family from India recently moved into my neighborhood. They plan to stay here at least a year.
7. I bought a new telescope. And I wanted to use it to study the moon. And a few of my friends said they wanted to use it with me.	7. I bought a new telescope for studying the moon. A few of my friends said they wanted to study the moon, too.
8. Computers have many purposes. They are used for banking. They are used for designing robots. They are used for making animated movies. And they have many other uses.	8. Computers have many uses. These include banking, designing robots, and making animated movies.

CLICHÉS

Writers who seek to be creative avoid phrases that seem to "write themselves." To put it differently, they won't touch clichés with a ten-foot pencil.

DIRECTIONS:
1. On the board, write a sentence containing a cliché:
   It's light as a feather.
2. Ask students to edit the sentence in a way that avoids the cliché. You might define "cliché" as "an overused phrase."
3. Have the students assist you as you edit the sentence:
   It's light as a hummingbird.
4. Explain that when writers use clichés, they give up their own voice. There are several ways to avoid this problem:
   - Create a new image or comparison, as was done by using the word "hummingbird."
   - Twist the cliché to surprise readers, as was done by changing "ten-foot pole" into "ten-foot pencil."
   - Present the information factually: "It weighs only a few ounces." This third option is the least creative, but it's better than using a cliché.

EXTENSION:
Make a bulletin board of clichés found in the media. Hint: You know it's a cliché if you can complete the sentence after hearing a few words.

Editing Examples: Clichés

Note: There is no one right way to change a cliché. The edited versions below are merely samples.

First Draft	Edited Draft
1. Avoid it like the plague.	1. Whatever you do, avoid it.
2. Its big as a house.	2. It's big as a jumbo jet.
3. The book bored me to tears.	3. Reading blank pages would be more interesting than reading this book.
4. The explosion was as bright the sun.	4. The explosion was as bright as a high-intensity streetlight.
5. This room is cold as ice.	5. The temperature here is 2 degrees Celsius.
6. The guppy is dead as a doornail.	6. The guppy is dead as a clipped toenail.
7. She's happy as a lark	7. She's happy as a smiley face.
8. Am I going. No way!	8. Am I going? Absolutely not.
9. That runner runs quick as a flash.	9. That runner broke the school record.
10. It's raining cats and dogs.	10. It's raining two inches an hour.
11. The bus was moving slow as a snail.	11. The bus was moving so slowly I could have gotten home faster by walking.
12. This side walk is smooth as silk.	12. This sidewalk is so smooth, when you roller skate on it you feel nothing.
13. They painted the house white as snow.	13. They painted the house white as blank computer paper.

COMMA SPLICES

Separate ideas belong in separate sentences, clearly set apart by a period. Joining two separate sentences with a comma creates a hard-to-read "comma splice" sentence.

DIRECTIONS:

1. On the board, write a comma splice example:

   I saw that movie, it was not scary.
2. Ask students to edit the sentence.
3. Have students assist you as you edit the sentence:

   I saw that movie. It was not scary.
4. Discuss the reason for the change. Merging two separate ideas can confuse readers. A comma does not give enough separation. It should be replaced by a period, by a semicolon, or by a conjunction ("and," "or," "but," "because").
5. Use the examples on the next page for more practice.

EXTENSION:

To help students become aware of the importance of creating distinct sentences, divide the class into small groups. Have each group write a collaborative story by taking turns adding a sentence at a time.

Editing Examples: Comma Splices

First Draft

1. There are 9 planets in the Solar System, they all travel around the sun.

2. Rhode island is the smallest U.S. state, alaska is the largest.

3. In the metric system, water boils at 100 degrees Celsius, it freezes at 0 degree.

4. Many english words are shortened forms of longer words, an example is "taxi," which comes from "taxicab."

5. The statue of liberty was created by a frenchman named Auguste Bartholdi, the sculptor used his Mother as the model.

6. Lemons are a good source of Vitamin C, because the juice can harm tooth enamel, rinse the mouth with water after drinking it.

7. David Bushnell invented the first military submarine, it was piloted by Ezra Lee during the Revolutionary War.

8. Paris is a town in Kentucky it was named by citizens grateful for the help france gave to america during the war for independence.

9. During the 19th century, feathers were used to make golf balls the feathers were stuff into leather bags and sewn up.

Edited Draft

1. There are nine planets in the solar system. They all travel around the sun.

2. Rhode Island is the smallest U.S. state. Alaska is the largest.

3. In the metric system, water boils at 100 degrees Celsius. It freezes at 0 degrees.

4. Many English words are shortened forms of longer words. An example is "taxi," which comes from "taxicab."

5. The Statue of Liberty was created by a Frenchman named Auguste Bartholdi. The sculptor used his mother as the model.

6. Lemons are a good source of vitamin C. Because the juice can harm tooth enamel, rinse the mouth with water after drinking it.

7. David Bushnell invented the first military submarine. It was piloted by Ezra Lee during the Revolutionary War.

8. Paris is a town in Kentucky. It was named by citizens grateful for the help France gave to America during the War for Independence.

9. During the 19th century, feathers were used to make golf balls. The feathers were stuffed into leather bags and sewn up.

CONTRACTION ERRORS

Contracted words are widely used. That's why contractions are responsible for so many misspellings.

DIRECTIONS:
1. On the board, write a sentence containing a contraction error:

Talk does'nt cook rice.

2. Ask students to edit the sentence.
3. Have students assist you as you edit the sentence:

Talk doesn't cook rice.

4. Explain that the apostrophe marks the spot where one or more letters have been omitted. The apostrophe does not mark the place where a space is omitted. When contracting the phrase "does not," the apostrophe doesn't go between the *s* and the *n*. Rather, it replaces the missing *o*.
5. Use the examples on the next page for more practice.

EXTENSION:
Have students make a bulletin board of newspaper headlines that contain contractions. The large-sized typography can help reinforce the placement of the apostrophes.

Editing Examples: Contraction Errors

First Draft	**Edited Draft**
1. Dont bite the hand that feeds you.	1. Don't bite the hand that feeds you.
2. Rome was'nt built in a day.	2. Rome wasn't built in a day.
3. The leopard cann't change his spots.	3. The leopard can't change his spots.
4. Where theres a will, theres a way.	4. Where there's a will, there's a way.
5. People who live in glass houses should'nt throw stones.	5. People who live in glass houses shouldn't throw stones.
6. When the wells dry, we know the worth of water.	6. When the well's dry, we know the worth of water.
7. Thats one small step for man, one giant leap for mankind.	7. That's one small step for man, one giant leap for mankind.
8. Dont count you're chickens before theyr'e hatched.	8. Don't count your chickens before they're hatched.
9. One swallow does'nt make a summer.	9. One swallow doesn't make a summer.
10. When fate hands us a lemon, lets try to make lemonade.	10. When fate hands us a lemon, let's try to make lemonade.
11. Courage is'nt freedom from fear; its being afraid and still going on.	11. Courage isn't freedom from fear; it's being afraid and still going on.
12. Your nothing but a pack of cards! said Alice.	12. "You're nothing but a pack of cards!" said Alice.
13. Its three oclock in the morning.	13. It's three o'clock in the morning.
14. Beware of anyone who wo'nt be bothered with details.	14. Beware of anyone who won't be bothered with details.

DANGLING PARTICIPLES

For clarity, writers should keep descriptive words near what they describe. Otherwise, sentences can be confusing or even unintentionally funny.

DIRECTIONS:
1. On the board, write a sentence containing a dangling participle. This is a sentence in which there is no word for the participle to describe:

Riding your bike, the seat was too high.

2. Ask students to edit the sentence.
3. Have students assist you as you edit the sentence:

Riding your bike, I found that the seat was too high.

4. Point out that the phrase "Riding your bike" seems to describe "the seat." But that's silly because a seat doesn't ride a bike. "Riding your bicycle" should refer to a person. That's why "I" was added to the sentence. Note that there are other ways to solve the problem:

I was riding your bike, but the seat was too high.

EXTENSION:
Have students create funny dangling-participle posters that raise everyone's consciousness about the problem.

Editing Examples: Danglers

First Draft	Edited Draft
1. Looking moldy, I did'nt eat the bread.	1. I didn't eat the moldy-looking bread.
2. Fearing the worst the spelling test, was easy.	2. Although I feared the spelling test, I found it easy.
3. Rowing acrost the lake, the house looked deserted.	3. The house looked deserted to me as I rowed across the lake.
4. While sleeping soundly, the bad nightmare waked me.	4. A nightmare woke me from a sound sleep. [Or: "While sleeping soundly, I was awakened by a nightmare."]
5. Covered with mud after the game, a shower cleaned me up.	5. Covered with mud after the game, I took a shower to clean up.
6. Wanting to makeup with my friend after our fight, an apology was in order.	6. Wanting to make up with my friend after our fight, I apologized.
7. Feeling hungry, a half filled cookie jar caught my attention.	7. I was hungry and noticed a half-filled cookie jar.
8. Sliding down the hill, the snow was smooth and hard.	8. I slid down the hill on the smooth, hard snow.
9. Looking everywhere, the box couldn't be found.	9. I looked everywhere for the box, but I couldn't find it.
10. Whistling loudly, my dog come running.	10. I whistled loudly, and my dog came running.
11. Bubbling on the stove, I turned off the burner.	11. I turned off the burner under the bubbling pot.

DISORGANIZED WRITING

Writers are told to "start at the beginning and go from there." Unfortunately, finding the beginning is often easier said than done.

DIRECTIONS:
1. Give each student, or pair of students, a copy of the picture story found on the next pages.
2. Ask students to arrange the pictures into a story that makes sense. Younger students might find the task easier if they first cut apart the panels and then physically arrange them. Note: There is no one right way to do it.
3. Have students outline the story, for example:

> Picture C. The weather turns nasty.
> Picture E. Weather forecasters study the storm.
> Picture B. The newspaper warns of danger.

4. Share the outlines orally.

EXTENSION:
For an all-text version of the activity, use the jumbled article on page 23. The correct sequence of paragraphs is: D, E, B, A, G, F, C.

Editing Example: Disorganized Report

The paragraphs below are jumbled. Put them into an order that tells the story.

From Pie to Sky: The Frisbee Story

A) In California, inventor Walter Morrison heard about flying saucers. It gave him an idea. Why not make a throwing toy that would cash in on the flying-saucer fad?

B) Soon the whole country was flying-saucer crazy. People began seeing flying saucers everywhere. Publishers brought out many books on the subject. Hollywood followed with science-fiction movies featuring flying saucers.

C) Over the years, hundreds of millions of plastic Frisbee discs have been sold around the world.

D) In the 1920s, the Frisbie Pie Company of Bridgeport, Connecticut, sold pies in tin pie plates. Students at nearby Yale University ate the pies and then used the tins in a throwing game called "Frisbie-ing." Skilled players could even get the tins to do tricks, like hovering or returning to the thrower.

E) Two decades later, in 1947, a Washington State businessman named Kenneth Arnold was flying his small plane near Mount Rainier when he spotted nine strange flying machines. Arnold told reporters that these mysterious objects looked like "upside down saucers."

F) Eventually, a California company called Wham-O bought Morrison's invention and made the toy popular across the country. When a salesperson from Wham-O heard about the Frisbie pie tins, the company decided to use the name for the plastic saucers, spelling it Frisbee instead of Frisbie.

G) Because Morrison knew that metal saucers could be dangerous, he decided to make his toy out of plastic, which was just becoming popular. He bought a molding machine and started making plastic "flying saucers," which he sold at fairs. He named his toy the Pluto Platter.

FACT ERRORS

Readers expect "true" facts. Even in fiction, the information about real things should be correct, unless the writer is creating a fantasy world in which you might find a spider with seven legs.

DIRECTIONS:
1. On the board, write a sentence with a fact error on a subject familiar to students. Include at least one mechanical error to make the fact problem less obvious:
> **September is the 8th month off the year.**
2. Ask students to edit the sentence.
3. Have students assist you as you edit the sentence:
> **September is the ninth month of the year.**
4. Discuss the changes, emphasizing that careful writers look up every fact they're not sure of.
5. Use the examples on the next page for more practice. You can also create fact errors about local sports teams, playground equipment, the weather ("Today it's snowing" when it's really raining), and room facts ("There are six lights on" when in fact there are four).

EXTENSION:
Give students sentences that require research to check the facts. For sample worksheets see pages 26 and 27.

Editing Examples: Fact Errors

First Draft	**Edited Draft**
1. Two times nineteen is fourty-eight.	1. Two times nineteen is thirty-eight.
2. The months spelled with the fewest letters is March.	2. The month with the fewest letters in its name is May.
3. Alphabetically, Monday is the first day of the week.	3. Alphabetically, Friday is the first day of the week.
4. Of the ten digits, just two of them—1 and 4—are formed using only straight lines.	4. Of the ten digits, just three of them—1, 4, and 7—are formed using only straight lines.
5. The letters *o*, *p*, *s*, and *t* can be used to spell only one word: "stop."	5. The letters *o*, *p*, *s*, and *t* can be used to spell five words: "stop," "pots," "spot," "tops," and "post." [Words formed from the same letters are called "anagrams."]
6. On a clock, the numbers 5 and 10 is directly opposite each other.	6. On a clock, the numbers 5 and 11 are directly opposite each other. [Or "...4 and 10..."]
7. The letters *l* and *m* are the middle letters in the alphabet.	7. The letters *m* and *n* are the middle letters in the alphabet.
8. Eight months have thirty one days.	8. Seven months have thirty-one days.
9. When you open a book written in English and look at the two facing pages the odd-numbered page will always be on left.	9. When you open a book written in English and look at the two facing pages, the odd-numbered page will always be on the right.
10. Of the twenty-six letters, none rhymes with the letter *i*.	10. Of the twenty-six letters, only *y* rhymes with the letter *i*.

Fact Checking: Sentences

If a sentence is factually correct, write "OK" in front of it.
If a sentence contains a fact error, cross out the error and
write in the correct fact. On the space marked "Source,"
name the book or person that gave you the information.

1. There are twenty-two states in Mexico.
Source_____

2. The words "pedestal" and "pedestrian" have the same root.
Source_____

3. The Mediterranean Sea is the world's largest sea.
Source_____

4. The Fahrenheit scale was developed by Daniel Fahrenheit.
Source_____

5. Ottawa is closer to the North Pole than Boston is.
Source_____

6. Shellac comes from pine trees.
Source_____

7. Basketball was invented in Springfield, Illinois.
Source_____

8. New York City was the first capital of the United States.
Source_____

9. The sun is closer to Earth in summer than in winter.
Source_____

10. The explosion of the Krakatoa volcano took place in 1882.
Source_____

11. The moon's diameter is one-half the length of Earth's
diameter.
Source_____

12. Dwight Eisenhower was the thirty-second U.S.
President.
Source_____

Fact Checking: Pictures

Each picture below contains one or more errors. Correct the errors by writing in the margin. On the line marked "Source," name the book or person that gave you the information.

Source _____   Source _____

Source _____   Source _____

HOMONYM MIX-UPS

Homonyms (also called "homophones") cause many spelling errors. Awareness is a key step in solving the problem.

DIRECTIONS:
1. On the board, write a sentence containing a homonym error:

    I like to right poetry.

2. Ask students to edit the sentence.
3. Have students assist you as you edit the sentence:

    I like to write poetry.

4. Explain that homonyms are "sound-alike" words that have different meanings. Because it's easy to mix up homonyms, writers need to be aware of the problem.
5. Use the examples on the next page for more practice.

EXTENSION:
To increase homonym awareness, have students create homonym riddles. These are fill-in-the-blank sentences that challenge readers or listeners to guess missing homonyms from the context given. For example:

    Look over _____ and you'll see the place where the dogs buried _____ bones. (there, their)

You might publish the students' riddles in a book to share with other classes and with parents. For a sampler of homonym riddles, see page 88.

Editing Examples: Homonyms

First Draft	Edited Draft
1. I ca'nt here you when you whisper.	1. I can't hear you when you whisper.
2. He asked if he could come to.	2. He asked if he could come, too.
3. They lost there dog.	3. They lost their dog.
4. Its going to be hot this summer.	4. It's going to be hot this summer.
5. What will you where to the party.	5. What will you wear to the party?
6. I borrowed for Library books.	6. I borrowed four library books.
7. Fix the break on your bike.	7. Fix the brake on your bike.
8. I sneezed because I have the flew.	8. I sneezed because I have the flu.
9. Theres a whole in my sock.	9. There's a hole in my sock.
10. I'd like a peace off cake.	10. I'd like a piece of cake.
11. Climbing stares is good exercise.	11. Climbing stairs is good exercise.
12. For dessert, I had a Sunday.	12. For dessert, I had a sundae.
13. The dog wagged it's tale.	13. The dog wagged its tail.
14. If your happy, smile.	14. If you're happy, smile.
15. Who's jacket is this.	15. Whose jacket is this?
16. I through the paper away.	16. I threw the paper away.
17. The batter hitted a fowl ball.	17. The batter hit a foul ball.
18. Whats the whether for tomorrow.	18. What's the weather for tomorrow?

INCONSISTENCIES

English contains many inconsistencies. For example, "OK" and "Okay" are both acceptable spellings. Nevertheless, because switching back and forth can distract readers, careful writers choose one way and stick to it

DIRECTIONS:
1. On the board, write a sentence with an inconsistency:
   > **I waved "Goodbye" to my dog and she wagged her tail "Goodby."**
2. Ask students to edit the sample.
3. Have students assist you as you edit the sentence:
   > **I waved "Goodbye" to my dog and she wagged her tail "Goodbye."**
4. Discuss the revision. Either spelling of goodbye is correct, but only one should be used in a single piece of writing. This is called being consistent. Writing that is not consistent can confuse or annoy readers.
5. In addition to spelling, review other inconsistencies:
   • Point of view: e.g., using second and third person
   • Style/formality: e.g., switching between "that's" and "that is"
   • Lettering: e.g., using upper- and lower-case letters in one title and all upper-case letters in another
6. Use the examples on the next page for more practice.

EXTENSION:
To raise consciousness about consistency traps, have students search the dictionary, looking for examples of words that can be spelled or pronounced in two ways. Share the examples on a bulletin board.

Editing Examples: Inconsistencies

First Draft	Edited Draft
1. My dentist appointment is at 3 P.M. and my music lesson at 5 p.m.	1. My dentist appointment is at 3 P.M. and my music lesson at 5 P.M. [Or "...3 p.m"..."5 p.m."]
2. At the party I saw Doctor Putnam and Dr. Barlow.	2. At the party I saw Dr. Putnam and Dr. Barlow.
3. During our vacation, we visited Dallas, TX, Flagstaff, AZ, and Los Angeles, California..	3. During our vacation, we visited Dallas, Texas, Flagstaff, Arizona, and Los Angeles, California. [Or: Dallas, TX, Flagstaff, AZ, and Los Angeles, CA.]
4. Last summer my family traveled to Florida. At the same time, my Cousin's family travelled to Alaska.	4. Last summer my family traveled to Florida. At the same time, my cousin's family traveled to Alaska.
5. Two of my favorite books are <u>Tuck Everlasting</u> and <u>A WRINKLE IN TIME</u>.	5. Two of my favorite books are <u>Tuck Everlasting</u> and <u>A Wrinkle in Time</u>.
6. Someone misplaced the coat of my sister and my father's keys.	6. Someone misplaced my sister's coat and my father's keys.
7. When people see a scary movie, sometimes you just want to close your eyes.	7. When people see a scary movie, sometimes they just want to close their eyes. [Or: "When you see...you just..."]
8. At the swim meet, I swam in lane number 1 and my friend swam in lane no. 3.	8. At the swim meet, I swam in lane number 1 and my friend swam in lane number 3.
9. <u>Journey to the Moon</u> is a CD-ROM that covers three topics: a) astronomy, b) rockets, and 3) science fiction.	9. <u>Journey to the Moon</u> is a CD-ROM that covers three topics: a) astronomy, b) rockets, and c) science fiction. [Or: "1)...2)...3)..."]
10. I like summer sports, e.g., swimming. I also like winter sports, for example, sledding.	10. I like summer sports, for example, swimming. I also like winter sports, for example, sledding.

MISMATCHED WORDS

Just as a well-dressed person wears matching items of clothing, a careful writer must make sure that the parts of a sentence fit together. This is called "agreement."

DIRECTIONS:
1. On the board, write a sentence that contains an agreement problem:

   I see many cloud.
2. Ask students to edit the sentence.
3. Have students assist you as you edit the sentence:

   I see many clouds.
4. Explain the reason for the change: Because "many" is a plural adjective, it requires a plural noun. If there were just one cloud, then the sentence might read:

   I see a cloud.
5. Go over other kinds of agreement problems:
   - Article-noun: I ate a (an) apple.
   - Subject-verb: My friends likes (like) bananas.
   - Noun-pronoun: Everyone must bring their (his or her) towel. (Or: "Everyone must bring a towel.")
6. Use the examples on the next page for more practice.

EXTENSION:
Students who speak English as a second language frequently have trouble with article-noun agreement. If you encounter this problem, you might prepare worksheets that provide intensive practice.

Editing Examples: Mismatched Words

First Draft	Edited Draft
1. No answer is also a anser.	1. No answer is also an answer.
2. One picture are worth a thousand word.	2. One picture is worth a thousand words.
3. A student can learn something new any time you believe you can.	3. A student can learn something new any time he believes he can. [Because "student" is a third-person subject, the pronoun must also be in the third person. To avoid using the masculine "he" to represent both genders while avoiding the awkward he/she construction, change the subject to plural: "People can learn something new any time they believe they can."]
4. This week I ate a pair, apple, and banana.	4. This week I ate a pear, an apple, and a banana.
5. On my street, there's 3 striped cats.	5. On my street, there are three striped cats.
6. Sandy is the only one of all my friends who play the piano.	6. Sandy is the only one of my friends who plays the piano.
7. These kind of games boar me.	7. These kinds of games bore me. [Or: "This kind of game bores me."]
8. One of the best way to learn a skill is to spend time with someone who has that skill.	8. One of the best ways to learn a skill is to spend time with someone who has that skill.
9. When my family was on vacation, they always ate to gether.	9. When my family was on vacation, we always ate together.
10. We was afraid of the lighting storm.	10. We were afraid of the lightning storm.

MISPLACED WORDS

There's an old saying: "A place for everything, and everything in its place." This is as true for words in a sentence as it is for tools in a toolbox.

DIRECTIONS:
1. On the board, write a sentence with a misplaced word or phrase:
   I rode my skateboard up the hill quickly.
2. Ask students to edit the sentence.
3. Have students assist you as you edit the sentence:
   I quickly rode my skateboard up the hill.
4. Explain that for clarity, writers should place modifiers (adverbs and adjectives) as close as possible to the words they modify. Also, it's usually best to put the subject near the beginning of the sentence.
5. Use the examples on the next page for more practice.

EXTENSION:
Have students write short essays about keeping things in order. They might write about a closet or drawer at home, a desk at school, or some other place where order is important.

Editing Examples: Misplaced Words

First Draft	Edited Draft
1. I dived in to the water awkwardly.	1. I awkwardly dived into the water.
2. Carelessly, into the kitchen I walked & cut myself, while slicing a tomato.	2. I walked into the kitchen and carelessly cut myself while slicing a tomato.
3. A long distance, I threw the ball.	3. I threw the ball a long distance.
4. Easily, the weight lifter, with a smile, pick up the heavy barbells.	4. With a smile, the weight lifter easily picked up the heavy barbells.
5. The dog, because he was happy to see me, run around in circles.	5. Because he was happy to see me, the dog ran around in circles.
6. I yelled to get the attention of the police officer loudly, but she didn't here me.	6. I yelled loudly to get the attention of the police officer, but she didn't hear me.
7. Under the brick, where no one was likely to find it, I left a message.	7. I left a message under the brick, where no one was likely to find it.
8. The baker spread the frosting on the birthdaycake smoothly.	8. The baker smoothly spread the frosting on the birthday cake.
9. Our school need new playground equipment desperately.	9. Our school desperately needs new playground equipment.
10. Please paint these boards, which will be used to build a children's playhouse, bright red.	10. Please paint these boards bright red. They'll be used to build a children's playhouse.
11. Steadily, the tightrope walker looked straight ahead and moved forward over the river.	11. The tightrope walker looked straight ahead and steadily moved forward over the river.
12. I arrived at school yesterday late.	12. Yesterday I arrived late at school.

PARAGRAPH PROBLEMS

There's only one widely followed paragraphing rule: In a story, start a new paragraph whenever a different character talks. In most other situations, writers intuitively decide where to give readers a break.

DIRECTIONS:
1. Reformat a short story or article with the paragraphing removed. Number the lines. (See the example on page 37 and the edited version on page 38.)
2. Duplicate the un-paragraphed material and give a copy to each student or to a pair of students.
3. Ask students to use the paragraph symbol, shown in the margin on this page, to indicate each place a paragraph should begin. To make the task easier, reveal the number of paragraphs in the original.
4. Have students assist you as you edit the material. This will be easier if you have an overhead projector.
5. Discuss the reasons for each paragraph break. Because even professional writers may disagree on where a paragraph break should occur, be prepared for differences.

EXTENSION:
Because coherence is a feature of strong paragraphs, sometimes present a paragraph with an extraneous sentence. Challenge students to delete it and explain why it doesn't fit. You'll find sample paragraphs on page 39.

Editing Example: Paragraphing

1.   **A Friend's Promise**

2.   Two friends, Elko and Ogbert, were hiking together.

3.   When they were about to enter a dark forest, Elko

4.   said to Ogbert, "I promise to help you if anything

5.   bad happens." Ogbert replied, "You can count on

6.   me, too." An hour later, they heard loud growling

7.   and turned to see a huge bear coming at them.

8.   Elko, who was a good climber, shinnied up a tree

9.   that was too thin for the bear to climb. "Quick, give

10.   me a hand," shouted Ogbert, but Elko kept climbing

11.   and never looked back. When Ogbert

12.   realized he could not get away, he fell down and

13.   pretended to be dead. The bear sniffed Ogbert, even

14.   nuzzling the man's ear for a moment. Ogbert was

15.   terrified, but didn't move. The bear, who preferred to

16.   go after live prey, soon lost interest and went off into

17.   the woods without hurting Ogbert. A few minutes

18.   later, Elko climbed down the tree and said, "It

19.   looked like the bear was talking to you. What did he

20.   say when he put his mouth next to your ear?"

21.   Ogbert answered, "He told me that I should be more

22.   choosy about who I hike with. He warned me not be

23.   friends with anyone who makes a promise to help

24.   but breaks it the first time help is needed."

Editing Example: Paragraphing

1.   **A Friend's Promise**

2. ¶Two friends, Elko and Ogbert, were hiking together.

3. When they were about to enter a dark forest, Elko

4. said to Ogbert, "I promise to help you if anything

5. bad happens." Ogbert re¶plied, "You can count on

6. me, too." An hour l¶ater, they heard loud growling

7. and turned to see a huge bear coming at them.

8. Elko, who was a good climber, shinnied up a tree

9. that was too thin for the bear to climb. "Qu¶ick, give

10. me a hand," shouted Ogbert, but Elko kept climbing

11. and never looked back. When O¶gbert

12. realized he could not get away, he fell down and

13. pretended to be dead. The bear sniffed Ogbert, even

14. nuzzling the man's ear for a moment. Ogbert was

15. terrified, but didn't move. The bear, who preferred to

16. go after live prey, soon lost interest and went off into

17. the woods without hurting Ogbert. ¶A few minutes

18. later, Elko climbed down the tree and said, "It

19. looked like the bear was talking to you. What did he

20. say when he put his mouth next to your ear?"

21. ¶Ogbert answered, "He told me that I should be more

22. choosy about who I hike with. He warned me not be

23. friends with anyone who makes a promise to help

24. but breaks it the first time help is needed."

Editing Examples: Paragraph Focus

Each of the following paragraphs has a sentence that doesn't belong.

In 1964, there was a serious coin shortage throughout the United States. To help solve the problem, a Wisconsin bank began manufacturing wooden nickels. Wisconsin had become a state in 1848. Business owners agreed to accept the nickels from customers. Nevertheless, when the U.S. Treasury Department heard about this scheme, it put a quick stop to it. The Treasury called the wooden coins "counterfeit money."

Malaria is a disease in which victims suffer high fevers and chills. The illness is caused by a microscopic parasite living in animal and human blood. The parasite is carried by mosquitoes, which suck up infected blood from people who have the disease and then inject the blood into healthy people. For many years, quinine, which comes from the bark of the cinchona tree, was the only treatment for malaria, but now new medicines are being used. Bark from different kinds of trees has many medical and non-medical uses.

Hoover Dam is one of the world's largest dams. It stands 726 feet (221 meters) tall, and 1,244 feet (379 meters) long. The dam, built near Las Vegas, blocks the Colorado River between Nevada and Arizona. Constructed between 1931 and 1936, it created Lake Mead, the largest reservoir in the United States. The word "reservoir," like many English words, comes from a French word. Hoover Dam was originally called Boulder Dam, but was renamed for President Herbert Hoover in 1948.

PASSIVE VOICE

In a sentence written in the passive voice, the subject receives the action. The passive voice is not an error, but it's wordier and less dramatic than the active voice.

DIRECTIONS:
1. If students aren't familiar with the two "voices," on the board write a passive-voice sentence and a corresponding active-voice version. Label each sentence:

Passive voice: I was kicked by the horse.
Active voice: The horse kicked me.

2. Explain that the passive voice consists of the helping verb "be" ("is," "was," "were," etc.) plus a participle and often a prepositional phrase ("by the horse") that names the source of the action. Point out that the active voice is more concise (uses fewer words) than the passive voice.
3. Write another passive-voice sentence on the board:

They were soaked by the rain.

4. Ask students to rewrite the sentence in the active voice.
5. Have students assist you as you edit the sentence:

The rain soaked them.

6. Use the examples on the next page for more practice.

EXTENSION:
Have students write a story two ways: first using as many passive constructions as they can, and then writing the story in the active voice. They should compare the two versions in terms of clarity, drama, and conciseness.

Editing Examples: Passive Voice

First Draft	Edited Draft
1. The ball was hitted by the batter.	1. The batter hit the ball.
2. The song was performed by the Chorus.	2. The chorus performed the song.
3. We were met by my freind.	3. My friend met us.
4. This book is liked by every one.	4. Everyone likes this book.
5. The wallet was return by a stranger.	5. A stranger returned the wallet.
6. The law was passed by the city council.	6. The city council passed the law.
7. The actors were cheered by the audience.	7. The audience cheered the actors.
8. Your hair need's to be combed.	8. Your hair needs combing. [Or: "Comb your hair."]
9. The tree was blown down by the wind.	9. The wind blew down the tree.
10. The potatoe was peeled by me.	10. I peeled the potato.
11. I was made fun off by them.	11. They made fun of me.
12. The fense was painted today.	12. Someone painted the fence today. [Note: When the subject isn't stated in the passive, the editor must add one.]
13. The fire was started by a arsonist.	13. An arsonist started the fire.
14. The son is circled by nine planet.	14. Nine planets circle the sun.
15. A long boarder is shared by Canada and the U.S.	15. Canada and the U.S. share a long border.

POSSESSIVE ERRORS

Although the rules for spelling possessive nouns and pronouns are straightforward, these words frequently cause problems.

DIRECTIONS:
1. On the board, write a sentence with a misspelled possessive:
> **This is Ralphs' book, not her's.**
2. Ask students to edit the sentence.
3. Have students assist you as you edit the sentence:
> **This is Ralph's book, not hers.**
4. Discuss the reasons for each change:
- To form the possessive of a singular noun ("Ralph") add 's.
- Possessive pronouns ("his," "her," "ours," etc.) never use an apostrophe.

As you discuss the changes, you might refer students to the rules for forming the possessive in the Editing Guide.
5. Use the examples on the next page for more practice.

EXTENSION:
Have students clip and post possessives found in newspaper headlines and advertisements.

Editing Examples: Possessive Errors

First Draft	Edited Draft
1. That old cars' horn is broke.	1. That old car's horn is broken.
2. The drawing show the witches hat.	2. The drawing shows the witch's hat. [Or: "...witches' hats."]
3. The boys lost there books.	3. The boys lost their books.
4. The girls speech went well.	4. The girl's speech went well.
5. All ladie's shoes is on sale.	5. All ladies' shoes are on sale.
6. The scared childrens shouts woke every-one.	6. The scared children's shouts woke everyone.
7. Where is the mens' room.	7. Where is the men's room?
8. My Friend lost his' keys.	8. My friend lost his keys.
9. Is this sweater yours'.	9. Is this sweater yours?
10. Who's book is this.	10. Whose book is this?
11. That glass is'nt her's.	11. That glass isn't hers.
12. The fox'es cries led us to it's home.	12. The fox's cries led us to its home.
13. Either this is her's or it's mine's.	13. Either this is hers or it's mine.
14. That idea was Our's.	14. That idea was ours.
15. Both baseball team's cheering sections screaming.	15. Both baseball teams' cheering sections were screaming.

PREFIX PROBLEMS

By learning to handle prefixes, students will be able to overcome many spelling mistakes.

DIRECTIONS:
1. On the board, write a sentence with prefix problems:
   Don't mispell words like ilegal.
2. Ask students to edit the sentence.
3. Have students assist you as you edit the sentence:
   Don't misspell words like illegal.
4. Present the simple rule that covers all words formed with prefixes: "When a prefix is added to a base word, letters are never dropped from either the prefix or the base word." Use the prefix mis to illustrate the rule:
   mis + take = mistake
Emphasize that the rule holds even when the prefix ends with the same letter that begins the base word:
   mis + spell = misspell (not "mispell")
5. Use the examples on the next page for more practice.

EXTENSION:
Have students use a dictionary to learn the meaning of prefixes such as ac, ad, al, il, im, in, mis, and un. They might also make etymological reports on words formed with prefixes.

Editing Examples: Prefix Problems

First Draft	Edited Draft
1. A word processor can help someone who's hand writing is ilegible.	1. A word processor can help someone whose handwriting is illegible. ["illegible" = "not legible"]
2. We expect imature behavior from baby's because they're not adults..	2. We expect immature behavior from babies because they're not adults. ["immature" = "not mature"]
3. The person arrested by the Police kept shouting I'm inocent.	3. The person arrested by the police kept shouting, "I'm innocent." ["innocent" = "not (a) wrong doer"]
4. In the libary, please avoid unecessary talking.	4. In the library, please avoid unnecessary talking. ["unnecessary" = "not necessary"]
5. My neice fell down into the water after making a mistep.	5. My niece fell into the water after making a misstep.
6. Who acused me of braking the radio.	6. Who accused me of breaking the radio? ["accuse" = "to move to a case or lawsuit"]
7. If your ilogical, you may end up with dangerous ideas.	7. If you're illogical, you may end up with dangerous ideas.
8. This is a nation made up off imigrants.	8. This is a nation made of immigrants.
9. The doctor used a imense needle to give me an injection.	9. The doctor used an immense needle to give me an injection.
10. Its unatural to never blink.	10. It's unnatural to never blink.
11. Is it ilegal to throw trash on the ground.	11. Is it illegal to throw trash on the ground?

PRONOUN PUZZLERS

Pronouns cause problems because they change meaning according to context. The word "it" can refer to a flea in one paragraph and to a jumbo jet in the next. The key to pronoun mastery is understanding the concept of the antecedent, the word that the pronoun refers to.

DIRECTIONS:
1. On the board, write a sentence with a pronoun error:
   A student should listen to their teacher.
2. Ask students to edit the sentence.
3. Have students assist you as you edit the sentence:
   A student should listen to his or her teacher.
4. Discuss the reason for the change. A pronoun must agree with its antecedent. Since "student" is singular, it takes a singular pronoun. Or, to avoid the awkward "his or her," the antecedent can be made plural.
5. Use the examples on the next page for more practice. These examples include two types of problems:
   - Unclear antecedent: The pronoun might refer to either of two words or to a missing antecedent. For a lesson on teaching antecedents, see page 89.
   - Wrong form of the pronoun: The pronoun might be in the subjective case ("I") though the context calls for the objective case ("me").

EXTENSION:
Have students rewrite a fable or other familiar story, changing the pronouns from third person ("he," "she," "it") to first person ("I") or vice versa.

Editing Examples: Pronouns

First Draft	Edited Draft
1. I would like to be a pilot but it can take a long time.	1. I would like to be a pilot but becoming one can take a long time.
2. The rocket was brought on a truck. It was very big.	2. The rocket was brought on a big truck. [Or: "The big rocket was brought on a truck."]
3. The band came on two buses. They were very noise.	3. The band came on two noisy buses. [Or: "The noisy band came on two buses."]
4. One must watch his step.	4. One must watch one's step. [When used to mean "a person," "one" should not be followed by a pronoun indicating either gender. A less formal version is "You must watch your step."]
5. Joel and Bart went to his home.	5. Joel and Bart went to Joel's home. [Or: "...Bart's home."]
6. That elephant was captured by a hunter when he was ten years old.	6. When the hunter was ten years old, he captured that elephant. [Or: "When the elephant was ten years old, he was captured by a hunter."]
7. My brother and me saw the movie.	7. My brother and I saw the movie. [This is easy to see if you omit the first part of the subject. No one—except Tarzan—would say "Me saw the movie."]
8. A big problem people have when training pets comes from their stubbornness.	8. People have trouble when training stubborn pets. [Or: "Stubborn people have trouble training pets."]

PUNCTUATION PITFALLS

Because punctuating is a rule-driven activity, you might wish to make a bulletin board of punctuation rules ahead of time. You'll find the rules in the Editing Guide, starting on page 78.

DIRECTIONS:

1. On the board, write a sentence that contains the three major punctuation errors: missing mark, extra mark, and wrong mark:

   Do you want, carrots potatoes, or celery.

2. Ask students to edit the sentence.

3. Have students assist you as you correct the sentence:

   Do you want carrots, potatoes, or celery?

4. Discuss the reasons for each change:

   • There's no reason for a comma after "want."

   • Put a comma after carrots to separate items in a series. Note: Some experts omit the comma before "and" or "or."

   • Change the final period to a question mark because the sentence asks a question.

5. Use the examples on the next page for more practice.

EXTENSION:

To heighten awareness of punctuation marks, try the Punctuation Theater activity described on page 50.

Editing Examples: Punctuation Pitfalls

First Draft	Edited Draft
1. The 4 seasons are spring summer fall and winter	1. The four seasons are spring, summer, fall, and winter.
2. I'd like to go to the movies but I ought to practice my music lesson first.	2. I'd like to go to the movies, but I ought to practice my music lesson first.
3. Give me liberty or give me death.	3. Give me liberty, or give me death.
4. If you can tell the difference between good advice and bad advice you dont need advice.	4. If you can tell the difference between good advice and bad advice, you don't need advice.
5. In side the old cabin by the creek I found a box filled with diamond.	5. Inside the old cabin by the creek, I found a box filled with diamonds.
6. I said imitating my grandmas voice no thank you Sally.	6. I said, imitating my grandma's voice, "No thank you, Sally."
7. The large yellow Bird flew west.	7. The large, yellow bird flew west.
8. According to The Best Body Book there are three bones in the ear the hammer the anvil and the stirrup.	8. According to The Best Body Book, there are three bones in the ear: the hammer, the anvil, and the stirrup.
9. Ouch that hurt.	9. Ouch, that hurt!
10. Some people are winners others are losers.	10. Some people seem to be born winners; others seem to be born losers. [The semicolon could be replaced with a period.]
11. I would never not in a million years do what you did.	11. I would never—not in a million years—do what you did.
12. No answer, is also an answer.	12. No answer is also an answer.

49

PUNCTUATION THEATER

This pantomime-like activity is designed to increase awareness of punctuation.

DIRECTIONS:

1. Teach players gestures for the major punctuation marks:
   - Period—Point a finger at the audience.
   - Comma—With the right hand, make a sweeping, curved gesture starting at waist level and stopping at the bottom of the downward swing.
   - Quotation marks—Raise both hands slightly above the head and pivot the hands twice in succession.
   - Exclamation point—Raise one hand, then chop it downward quickly. Follow this by a period gesture—pointing a finger at the audience.
   - Semicolon—Make the period sign, rapidly followed by the comma sign.
   - Colon—Make two period gestures, one above the other.
   - Dash—Point one hand toward the audience and move it from one side to the other.

Of course, students can create their own punctuation gestures.

2. Divide the class into pairs.

3. Assign each pair a short text that contains several kinds of punctuation. Or have the students find or write their own text.

4. Have students rehearse their pieces. One student reads the piece slowly, while the other student dramatizes each punctuation mark.

5. Present the pantomimes for the class to enjoy.

EXTENSION:

For additional fun, have the students create sound effects to go with each mark. These effects can be performed by the mime or by a third member of the troupe.

Punctuation Gestures

period

comma

quotation marks

exclamation point

semicolon

dash

REDUNDANCIES

One of the surest ways to bore readers is to repeat something.

DIRECTIONS:
1. On the board, write a sentence that includes a redundancy:

The alarm rang at 6 a.m. in the morning.
2. Ask students to edit the sentence.
3. Have students assist you as you edit the sentence:

The alarm rang at 6 a.m.
4. Discuss the change. Because "a.m." means "in the morning," there is no reason to include both expressions. Point out that the sentence might also have been edited:

The alarm rang at six in the morning.
5. Use the examples on the next page for more practice.

EXTENSION:
While redundancy is a problem in writing, in some situations it's a plus. An example is a multi-engine plane. When one engine goes bad, the other engine or engines can keep the aircraft flying. Ask students to report on examples of useful redundancy at home or school, or in a product such as the family car.

Editing Examples: Redundancies

First Draft	Edited Draft
1. I ran from the big giant.	1. I ran from the giant. [Are there any "small giants?"]
2. I had a scary night mare.	2. I had a nightmare. [If it were the scariest of all nightmares, the sentence might read: "I had the scariest..."]
3. Keep away from that hot fire.	3. Keep away from that fire. [Can there be a "cold" fire?]
4. I used sticky glue to build this model.	4. I used glue to build this model.
5. The clown stepped into the cold wet dirty water.	5. The clown stepped into the cold, dirty water.
6. I fell down off the ladder.	6. I fell off the ladder. [Falling is always "down," except for astronauts.]
7. My ant works in a tall skyscraper.	7. My aunt works in a skyscraper.
8. Lets cooperate together.	8. Let's cooperate.
9. A strong gale bended the trees.	9. A gale bent the trees.
10. I took a tiny nible.	10. I took a nibble.
11. The stranger spoke in a quiet whisper.	11. The stranger spoke in a whisper. [Or: "The stranger whispered."]
12. Would you repeat that again.	12. Would you repeat that?
13. The two twins Bob and Sam came.	13. The twins, Bob and Sam, came.
14. The young puppy growled.	14. The puppy growled.

RUN-ON SENTENCES

Clear writing requires separating words and ideas. To teach this concept, write an un-spaced sentence on the board:

Canyoureadthissentenceeasily?

After students decode the message, point out that sentences, like words, must begin and end crisply.

DIRECTIONS:

1. On the board, write a run-on sentence:
   My friend plays the tuba she's good at it.
2. Ask the students to edit the sentence.
3. Have students assist you as you edit the sentence:
   My friend plays the tuba. She's good at it.
4. Explain the changes:
   • The period after "tuba" marks the end of the first sentence.
   • "She" is capitalized because it starts the next sentence.
5. Use the examples on the next page for more practice.

EXTENSION:

To help students notice sentence separation, have them count the sentences in a piece of writing. A related strategy is to ask students to write a story or description in a set number of sentences.

Editing Examples: Run-on Sentences

First Draft	**Edited Draft**
1. The first woman in space was a russian cosmonaut named Valentina Terreshkoe the first female American astronaut was Sally Ride.	1. The first woman in space was a Russian cosmonaut named Valentina Terreshkoe. The first female American astronaut was Sally Ride.
2. "Hippopotamus" means "river horse," but hippos arent horses there actually related to pigs.	2. "Hippopotamus" means "river horse," but hippos aren't horses. They're actually related to pigs.
3. Half the time the moon is visible at night the other 1/2 of the time it shines during the way.	3. Half the time the moon comes out at night. The other half of the time it shines during the day.
4. The pacific ocean is one of 5 oceans in the world the other three are the atlantic the indian the arctic and the antarctic.	4. The Pacific Ocean is one of four oceans in the world. The other three are the Atlantic, the Indian, and the Antarctic.
5. The first bicycle was made off wood and did'nt have pedals riders made it go by pushing the ground with their feet.	5. The first bicycle was made of wood and didn't have pedals. Riders made it go by pushing the ground with their feet.
6. Young bats are blind & helpless at birth three weeks later they can fly.	6. Young bats are blind and helpless at birth. Three weeks later they can fly.
7. Skin color is caused by melanin freckles are small patches of this light sensitive material.	7. Skin color is caused by melanin. Freckles are small patches of this light-sensitive material.
8. There are more than twenty million investors in the United States more than half are women.	8. There are more than twenty million investors in the United States. More than half are women.
9. Where did the Secret Service get its start President Lincoln began it as a group meant to stop counterfeiting during the Civil war.	9. Where did the Secret Service get its start? President Lincoln began it as a group meant to stop counterfeiting during the Civil War.

SENTENCE FRAGMENTS

All the king's horses and all the king's men couldn't put Humpty Dumpty together again. On the other hand, with a little practice, students should have an easy time turning sentence fragments into meaningful sentences.

DIRECTIONS:
1. One the board, write a sentence fragment:
 The two lively monkeys.
2. Ask students to edit the fragment. Because they'll have to guess at the meaning, expect many solutions.
3. Have students assist you as you edit the fragment. Several possibilities are:
 The two lively monkeys are TV stars.
 I saw two lively monkeys.
4. Explain that a sentence fragment lacks a subject (what the sentence is about) or a predicate (information about the subject) or both.
5. Use the examples on the next page for more practice. Some involve adding information. Others require joining a fragment with another fragment or with a complete sentence.

EXTENSION:
After students learn to deal with fragments, you might discuss two acceptable uses of fragments: as titles (*Beauty and the Beast*) and in dialogue:
 "What's that?" I asked my friend.
 "A surprise."

Editing Examples: Sentence Fragments

Because sentence fragments don't clearly suggest a single message, students will have to invent solutions. Therefore, expect a variety of responses.

First Draft	**Edited Draft**
1. In my opinion the most important reason for smileing.	1. In my opinion, the most important reason for smiling is to make other people feel like smiling.
2. I didn't want to go. On the other hand.	2. On the other hand, I didn't want to go. [Or: "I didn't want to go. On the other hand, I had to, because I promised I would."]
3. Sliding acrost the ice.	3. Sliding across the ice can be scary. [Or: "Sliding across the ice, I banged into a pole."]
4. My dad was talking in its sleep. And snoring.	4. My dad was talking in his sleep and snoring.
5. When it gets really freezing cold at night.	5. When it gets freezing cold at night, I like to sit in front of a fire.
6. My neighbor, whose always been kind to me.	6. My neighbor, who's always been kind to me, is moving away.
7. Because ridding bicycle can be dangerous. Riders ought to wear helmet.	7. Because riding a bicycle can be dangerous, riders ought to wear helmets.
8. In the first chapter of a book, about the biography story of Thomas Edison.	8. In the first chapter of the biography of Thomas Edison, you'll learn about Edison's education.
9. I drew a picture. Which didn't come out the way I wanted.	9. I drew a picture, which didn't come out the way I wanted.

SLOW STARTS

Just as first impressions are important, so are the first few words of a story or a report. The opening—also called "the lead"—can turn on or turn off one's readers.

DIRECTIONS:
1. On the board, write a boring lead:

> **This report is called Tooth Decay and it will tell you about tooth decay.**

2. Ask students to write a more creative lead for the same material. Point out that there is no one right way to do it.
3. Have several students share their revised leads on the board while you present your revision. One possibility:

> **Help! We're your teeth. If you don't take care of us, how can we take care of you?**

4. Discuss the classic kinds of beginnings that can be used instead of "Once upon a time." These include:
   - Asking a question
   - Describing a dramatic action
   - Giving a surprising fact or opinion
   - Quoting a character or an expert (dialogue lead)
   - Personifying an object

Humor is another way to win over an audience.
5. Use the examples on the next page for more practice.

EXTENSION:
Have students collect or create examples of the different kinds of leads. They can share these on a group bulletin board.

Editing Examples: Slow Starts

There's no one right way to revise a lead. What's important is making sure that the first words grab readers and move them toward the subject of the piece.

First Draft	Edited Draft
1. I'm going to tell you about what the first trip to mars will be like.	1. Three. Two. One. Blastoff. We're on the first rocket to Mars. Hold onto your space helmets. This is going to be a thrilling ride.
2. Once upon a time, something very unusual happened. there was a talking base ball, and it got into so much trouble, in the end it had to leave town.	2. My name is Stitches. You might think that's a strange name for a person. I agree, but I'm not a person. I'm a baseball, a talking baseball.
3. The name of the book I'm going to report on is How to Be an Inventor. It tells how you can invent toys and games and gadgets and thinks like that.	3. Did you ever get an idea for a new toy, game or gadget? It's not easy to follow through and create a new product, but there is a book that can help you do that. It's called How to Be an Inventor.
4. Digestion is the process by which food is turned into forms that the body can use.	4. "Chew your food." That's what your mom or dad has told you a million times. It's good advice. Thoroughly chewing your food is important for digestion.
5. In recent years, pigs have become more and more popular as pets.	5. What do you think of when you hear the word "pig"? Do you think of bacon or mud? If you do, you're not one of the thousands of people who keep pigs as pets.
6. This story starts when a stranger on a horse rode into town at midnight and shouted that a flood was coming. The stranger warned everybody to run.	6. "Wake up!" shouted the stranger, still in the saddle. "A flood is coming. You need to run to safety. Do it now!"

TENSE TROUBLES

There are two kinds of tense errors: wording mistakes ("brang" for "brought" or "I seen" for "I saw") and inconsistencies (randomly mixing past and present in a story or essay).

DIRECTIONS:

1. On the board, write a sentence that contains both kinds of tense errors:

> **Yesterday, I been in the supermarket when my friend walks in.**

2. Ask students to edit the sentence.
3. Have students assist you as you edit the sentence:

> **Yesterday, I was in the supermarket when my friend walked in.**

4. Discuss the two kinds of errors:
   - The first-person past tense of "to be" is "was."
   - Because the first part of the sentence is in the past tense, the second part should also be in the past tense.

5. Use the examples on the next page for more practice.

EXTENSION:

Students may have trouble forming the past tense of irregular verbs ("I seen him"). A simple exercise is looking up the parts in a dictionary. You'll find a short list of irregular verbs in the margin. For a longer list, see *Ten-Minute Grammar Grabbers* (Monday Morning Books).

Editing Examples: Tense

First Draft	Edited Draft
1. I have ate macaroni many time.	1. I have eaten macaroni many times.
2. Next wednesday, I visit my Aunt.	2. Next Wednesday, I will visit my aunt.
3. Our neighbors always be nice to me.	3. Our neighbors always are nice to me.
4. Two year ago, a storm blows down are garage.	4. Two years ago, a storm blew down our garage.
5. After my leg was broke, I wore a cast for a Month.	5. After my leg was broken, I wore a cast for a month.
6. Yesterday, because the whether is nice, we went to the beach.	6. Yesterday, because the weather was nice, we went to the beach.
7. I been tired all week because I couldnt sleep.	7. I have been tired all week because I couldn't sleep.
8. Then I asked "who brang the paper cup."	8. Then I asked, "Who brought the paper cup?"
9. The batter hitted the ball up over the fence.	9. The batter hit the ball over the fence.
10. The money was stole from off my desk.	10. The money was stolen from my desk.
11. No one seen what happened.	11. No one saw what happened.
12. It were cold last night.	12. It was cold last night.

TRITE TITLES

A dramatic title can hook readers' interest and prepare them to better understand a piece of writing

DIRECTIONS:
1. Choose a poem, a short story, or a short article to read aloud. (See the examples on the next page.)
2. On the board, write the trite title for the read-aloud item.
3. Read the piece aloud.
4. Discuss why the title is weak. Possible defects are:
   • Too general—It could fit many pieces of writing.
   • Unoriginal—It's been used before.
   • Vague—It doesn't create a mental picture.
   • Unrelated—It doesn't fit the work.
5. Have students, alone or with a partner, brainstorm a list of more interesting titles, then choose the best. If time permits, students should write a sentence or two explaining what's good about the new title.

EXTENSION:
When students produce their own stories or reports, divide the class into pairs. Have each student suggest an alternate title for his or her partner's written work.

Editing Examples: Trite Titles

Nonfiction

Birds
Can a bird fly backwards? If it's a hummingbird, yes. This tiny flier, which flaps its wings up to 75 times a second, can hover, travel sideways, and even fly backwards. Like a helicopter, it can rotate the angle of its wings, making it more agile than other birds.

Trees
Many people think that forest fires are bad, but fire is part of nature. For example, the cones of certain pine trees release their seeds only after being heated in a forest fire.

Spiders
Although a spider web tears easily, the silk spun out by the spider is the strongest thread in nature. It breaks easily only because it's so thin. For its size, it's actually stronger than steel.

Braille
Born in 1809, Louis Braille was blinded at age three. In those days, blind people often became beggars. But Louis' parents sent him to a special school. There, he heard about a complex touch code invented by a soldier for reading messages at night. Braille soon developed a simpler six-dot code. At first the government refused to support his method, but eventually it became the standard alphabet for millions of blind people.

Fiction

A Fable
As the north wind began to blow, a porcupine looked for a cozy place to spend the winter. After a few days, he found a cave in which lived a family of snakes. Because they seemed friendly, he asked them if he could move in with them. They said, "Certainly."

However, there wasn't much room inside the cave, and the snakes soon discovered that the porcupine's quills constantly stabbed them.

Finally, one of the snakes said to the porcupine, "We're sorry, but you'll have to move out. With you in here, it's impossible for us to get a good night's rest."

"I'm not moving," said the porcupine indignantly. "I'm satisfied with this cave. If you don't like it, you can leave."

Moral: Be careful how you choose your friends.

Another Fable
A farmer owned an excellent hen that laid an egg every day. Most people would be happy to have such an egg-layer, but the farmer wasn't satisfied. He decided to feed the hen twice as much so that the bird would lay two eggs a day. Unfortunately, the extra grain made the hen so fat that it no longer laid any eggs.

Moral: Don't be greedy.

UN-PARALLEL LISTS

Many sentences contain lists, for example, "life, liberty, and the pursuit of happiness." Sentences with lists are easier to read if the items have a single grammatical form. This is known as "being parallel."

DIRECTIONS:
1. On the board, write a sentence with an un-parallel list:
   Who likes reading, eating, and to laugh?
2. Ask students to edit the sentence.
3. Have students assist you as you edit the sentence:
   Who likes reading, eating, and laughing?
4. Discuss the reason for the change. Explain that lists make more sense when each word or phrase has the same form. Point out that there are other parallel versions:
   Who likes to read, to eat, and to laugh?
Note that items in a list should be separated by a comma.
5. Use the examples on the next page for more practice.

EXTENSON:
Have students brainstorm lists to deepen their understanding of parallelism. Some topics are:
   • "My Favorite Activities": reading, swimming, etc.
   • "Adjectives That Fit Me": careful, funny, etc.
   • "Plural Nouns in My Life": shoes, shirts, books, etc.

-PARK RULES-

1. No skateboarding.

2. Do not play your radio loudly.

3. You should not throw trash on the ground.

Editing Examples: Un-Parallel Lists

First Draft	**Edited Draft**
1. I can bike swim, and playing tennis.	1. I can bike, swim, and play tennis. [Note: Some writing experts leave out the comma before the "and."]
2. My dad drinks coffee and cold juice.	2. My dad drinks coffee and juice. [Or: "My dad drinks hot coffee and cold juice."]
3. I put on red shoes, green pant & a hat.	3. I put on red shoes, green pants, and an orange hat.
4. I can meet you on tuesday thursday or on friday.	4. I can meet you on Tuesday, Thursday, or Friday. [Or: "I can meet you on Tuesday, on Thursday, or on Friday."]
5. Baseball, football, and games like that can lead to friendships that last a Lifetime.	5. Games like baseball and football can lead to friendships that last a lifetime.
6. Don't laugh, cry, or other noises.	6. Don't laugh, cry, or make other noises.
7. The Tigers, the Broncos, and Dolphins are teams with animal names.	7. The Tigers, the Broncos, and the Dolphins are teams with animal names.
8. Practice or you must leave the team.	8. Practice or leave the team. [Or: "You must practice or you must leave the team."]
9. First I did twenty push-ups, and number two, I did 28 sit-ups.	9. First I did twenty push-ups, and second I did twenty-eight sit-ups.
10. Here's the chores we must do: 1) wash the dishes, 2) sweep the floor, and C) make the beds.	10. Here are the chores we must do: 1) wash the dishes, 2) sweep the floor, and 3) make the beds.

WEAK WORDS

Just as "uhs" can annoy listeners, "filler words"—such as "very"—may distract readers.

DIRECTIONS:
1. On the board, write a sentence that contains a weak word and underline it:

A spider's thread is <u>very</u> sticky.

2. Explain that words like "very" add little to a sentence. Usually they should be cut or replaced by a more precise or dramatic expression.
3. Ask students to replace "very" with a stronger word or phrase. Make sure they know that there is no one right way to do it.
4. Have students share their revisions orally. One possible version is:

A spider's thread is stickier than art glue.

5. Use the examples on the next page for more practice.

EXTENSION:
Post a list of weak words (see the list in the margin) and challenge students to write a story or article without using any of the words.

Weak Words

bad
basic
bit
definitely
fantastic
good
great
kind of
lots
neat
nice
really
so
special
thing
very

Editing Examples: Weak Words

There's no one right way to edit these drafts. Also, students will need to make up details for their edited drafts.

First Draft	Edited Draft
1. My report gives the basic facts about Spiders.	1. My report gives five important facts about spiders.
2. I feel bad.	2. I have a pain in my left wrist.
3. I ate a bit off candy.	3. I ate two pieces of candy.
4. This is definitely a good book.	4. The librarian recommends this book.
5. I saw a real scary movie yesterday	5. I saw a scary movie yesterday.
6. That was a good Article.	6. That article made me want to learn more about dinosaurs.
7. I had a great time at there party.	7. I enjoyed dancing at their party.
8. That is an incredible team.	8. That team won ten games in a row.
9. Im kind of hunger.	9. I'm hungry.
10. I played lots of Soccer last summer.	10. I played soccer daily last summer.
11. Thats a neat car.	11. That's a 1918 Ford.
12. I had a nice dream last nite.	12. Last night I dreamed I was a genius.
13. You dance pretty well.	13. You dance better than I do.
14. Theyr'e taking a special class.	14. They're taking a class in cooking.

WORD REPETITIONS

Accidentally repeating a word in a sentence can distract or even annoy readers.

DIRECTIONS:
1. On the board, write a sentence that contains an accidental word repetition:
   I fear that you have a fear of kittens.
2. Ask students to edit the sentence. You might focus their attention on the repetition.
3. Have students assist you as you edit the sentence:
   I worry that you have a fear of kittens.
Explain that unintended repetitions can distract or confuse readers. In the revision, "worry" is a synonym for "fear," a word with almost the same meaning. Point out that there are other ways to solve this kind of problem, for example:
   You seem to have a fear of kittens.
4. Discuss some of the ways to avoid repetitions:
   • Using a pronoun: "Here's the cat *that* tickled me."
   • Using an antonym or negative phrase: "I stood still. I did *not move.*"
   • Replacing a general word with a specific term: "I read a good book last week, a suspense *novel.*"
5. Use the examples on the next page for more practice.

EXTENSION:
Use the Finding Synonyms and Finding Antonyms worksheets, pages 70 and 71, to give students practice in the art of finding alternatives to a repeated word.

Editing Examples: Repetitions

First Draft	**Edited Draft**
1. On her trip to the lake last Fall my cousin tripped and broke her leg.	1. On her visit to the lake last fall, my cousin tripped and broke her leg.
2. I had a dream in which I had a bike.	2. I dreamed I had a new bike.
3. That noise from the highway is an unpleasant noise.	3. That roaring from the highway is an unpleasant noise.
4. I needed some money for shoping but I didn't have any money.	4. I needed some money for shopping but I was broke.
5. My friend and I am writing a paper about butterflys and I think its going to be a useful paper.	5. My friend and I are writing about butterflies, and I think it's going to be a useful paper. [Or: "...and I think it's going to be a useful report."]
6. There are many reason for owning a dog but the most important reason is companionship.	6. There are many reasons for owning a dog, but the most important is companionship. [Or: "...but at the top of my list is companionship."]
7. I hurt my side when I fell on the sidewalk.	7. I hurt my side when I fell on the walk.
8. Sometimes there isn't even time to get everything done.	8. Occasionally, there isn't even time to get everything done. [Or: "Sometimes I'm so busy, I can't get everything done."]
9. When I looked at the sky I saw a skywriter.	9. When I looked up, I saw a skywriter. [Or: "When I looked up at the sky, I saw an airplane using smoke to write a message."]
10. Don't promise you'll do it and then break your promise.	10. Don't promise one thing and then do another. [Or: "Don't break your promise."]

Finding Synonyms

Write one or more synonyms for each word. If two words are synonyms, they have nearly the same meaning. Use a dictionary, a thesaurus, or your memory. It's OK to use a phrase as a synonym. For example, a "cafeteria" might be called "an eating place."

animal

big

clothing

doctor

exciting

family

fast

flag

friend

good

happy

help

intelligent

money

nice

people

school

story

Finding Antonyms

Write one or more antonyms for each word. Antonyms are words or phrases with opposite meanings. Use a dictionary, a thesaurus, or your memory. It's OK to use a phrase as an antonym. For example, an antonym for "serious" could be "acting like a clown."

brave

calm

cautious

dangerous

easy

grateful

helpful

hero

honest

industrious

legal

loose

noisy

respect

shout

sick

smooth

spend

WORDINESS

"Simplify, simplify," said Henry Thoreau. He didn't mean that writers should be simple-minded, but rather that they should focus on essentials.

DIRECTIONS:
1. On the board, write a wordy sentence:
   > **The activity of science is really interesting to many people.**
2. Ask students to cut or reword the sentence so that the same idea is conveyed with fewer words.
3. Have students assist you as you edit the sentence:
   > **Science interests many people.**
4. Discuss the reason for each change:
   - The first three words are not needed because science is an activity.
   - Turning an adjective ("interesting") into a verb ("interests") usually saves several words.
   - An intensifier such as "really" is often fluff.
5. Use the examples on the next two pages for more practice.

EXTENSION:
For more practice, have students revise the wordy business letter of page 75.

Editing Examples: Wordiness

Because conciseness is a matter of style, there usually will be more than one way to reword each example.

First Draft	**Edited Draft**
1. It goes without saying that the grass need cutting.	1. The grass needs cutting. [If it goes without say, why say it?]
2. It seems that Winter has come.	2. Winter has come.
3. It is my belief that exercise improves ones health.	3. I believe that exercise improves one's health.
4. There are some animals that shouldn't be kept as pets.	4. Some animals shouldn't be kept as pets.
5. I certainly am upset, about the noise.	5. I am upset about the noise. [Or: "The noise upsets me."]
6. I thanked each and every person.	6. I thanked each person. [Or: "I thanked everyone."]
7. We sang, dance, talked, and etc.	7. We sang, danced, talked, etc. [Or: "We sang, danced, and talked."]
8. He has not got any money.	8. He has no money.
9. She is someone who cares.	9. She cares.
10. I hid inside of the closet.	10. I hid inside the closet.
11. I went on a fishing trip, which began 2 day ago.	11. I went fishing two days ago.
12. I read up until 8:30 p.m.	12. I read until 8:30 p.m.
13. The process of gift-wrapping can be creative.	13. Gift-wrapping can be creative.

Editing Examples: Wordiness

First Draft	Edited Draft
14. The fact that the book was damaged means I had to pay a fine.	14. Because the book was damaged, I had to pay a fine.
15. Some of the books in the library contain misinformation	15. Some books in the library contain misinformation.
16. No-thing has been done as yet.	16. Nothing has been done yet.
17. What kind off atree is this.	17. What kind of tree is this?
18. The game of baseball is played around the world.	18. Baseball is played around the world. ["Baseball" is a game, hence "The game of baseball" is redundant.]
19. The study of astronomy deals with vast distances.	19. Astronomy deals with vast distances.
20. The telling of gossip can really destroy friendships.	20. Gossip can destroy friendships.
21. I fell down on the ground.	21. I fell on the ground.
22. It was the babys crying that kept us up last night.	22. The baby's crying kept us up last night.
23. It was the Zuffmobile company that introduced lighted seats.	23. The Zuffmobile Company introduced lighted seats.
24. Hopefully, this new switch should solve the problem.	24. This new switch should solve the problem.
25. In terms of noise, this car is quieter then that one.	25. This car is quieter than that one.
26. I am very worried about the flood.	26. I am worried about the flood. [Or: "The flood worries me."]

Editing Examples: Wordiness

1.   2950 Neilson Way

2.   Santa Monica, CA 90405

3.   March 20, 1996

4.

5.   Irwin Hill

6.   Monday Morning Multimedia

7.   P.O. Box 1680

8.   Palo Alto, CA 94302

9.

10.   Dear Mr. Hill:

11.   I am at this time very much interested in the

12.   purchasing of your CD-ROM, which is entitled by the

13.   name "How to Be an Inventor." That sounds like a very

14.   good and useful project.

15.   For a very long time now I have wanted to become a

16.   person who invents things. I have a lot of really terrific

17.   ideas for new inventions.

18.   As soon as possible, could you please send to me

19.   more information that you have about your CD-ROM

20.   product right away?

21.   Thanks a lot for your very kind help in this matter

22.   which means a lot to me.

23.   Sincerely,

24.

25.

26.   Larry Howard

WRONG WORDS

"The difference between the right word and the almost right word," said Mark Twain, "is the difference between lightning and the lightning bug." Learning to value such distinctions is a key step towards literacy.

DIRECTIONS:
1. On the board, write a sentence with a wording error:
   In a hurry, I actually flew down the street.
2. Ask students to edit the sentence.
3. Have students assist you as you correct the sentence:
   In a hurry, I ran like a jaguar.
4. Discuss the changes. "Actually" means "really." You might also review the major kinds of wording errors:
   - Omitting a word
   - Using a nonstandard word such as "irregardless"
   - Choosing the wrong form, for example, an adjective where an adverb is needed ("slow" instead of "slowly")
   - Using the wrong homonym ("there" instead of "their")
   - Confusing similar words ("emigrate," "immigrate")
5. Use the examples on the next page for more practice.

EXTENSION:
Have students give presentations on words that cause problems. Their reports might include definitions, sample sentences, and even pictures. You'll find a list of troublesome words starting on page 93.

Editing Examples: Wrong Words

First Draft	**Edited Draft**
1. The dr. gave me a flu shot.	1. The doctor gave me a flu shot.
2. My room is more neater than it use to be.	2. My room is neater than it used to be.
3. That new machine digs more quick then the old one.	3. That new machine digs more quickly than the old one.
4. Irregardless off what happens, I'll be your friend for ever.	4. Regardless of what happens, I'll be your friend forever. ["Of" and "off" are frequently confused.]
5. I met Ralph, Frances, etc. at the library.	5. I met Ralph, Frances, and other friends at the library. ["Etc." means "and other things." It should not be used when referring to human beings.]
6. Neither Sheldon or Sandra is coming.	6. Neither Sheldon nor Sandra is coming. [Use "either/or" or "neither/nor."]
7. We divided the prize money between Sarah, Nancy, Simon.	7. We divided the prize money among Sarah, Nancy, and Simon. ["Between" means "by twos."]
8. I fell off of my bicycle.	8. I fell off my bicycle.
9. The way he looked at me he inferred that I should try again.	9. The way he looked at me implied that I should try again.
10. When I said "I can't help you," he goes "You better."	10. When I said "I can't help you," he replied "You better."
11. Because the path is slippery, walk careful.	11. Because the path is slippery, walk carefully.

EDITING GUIDE

Apostrophe: A punctuation mark ' used in spelling.
1. Use an apostrophe to mark where letters are deleted to form a contraction:

do not = don't

2. Use an apostrophe to form possessive nouns:

The dog's collar is missing.

Bracket: A punctuation mark [ ] used to enclose words added to a passage by another writer. In the following example, the bracketed words translate the opening words of Abraham Lincoln's Gettysburg Address:

"Four score and seven years ago" [87 years ago]...

Capital letter: A letter in the form of A, B, C, D rather than a, b, c, d.
1. Capitalize the first word of a sentence:

My name is Sarah.

2. Capitalize the first word in a quotation, even if it does not begin the sentence:

Rumpelstiltskin said, "You'll never guess my name."

3. Capitalize proper nouns, the names of particular people, places, and things:

I'm going to Virginia to see Mount Vernon, George Washington's home.

4. Capitalize the first word in a title and every other important word:

"The Family That Owned a Million Puppies"

Cliché: An overused word or phrase.

Colon: A punctuation mark : used to set apart words or phrases.
1. End the greeting in a formal letter with a colon:

Dear Ms. Smathers:

2. Use a colon before a list:

I like three fruits: apples, bananas, and cherries.

3. Use a colon to introduce an important word, phrase, or sentence:

I have one piece of advice for you: Tell the truth!

Editing Guide

Comma: A punctuation mark , used to separate words and word groups.

1. Use a comma to separate items in a list:
> Meet Kevin, Lacy, and Tina.

2. Use a comma with "and," "but," or "or" in a compound sentence:
> I like scuba diving, but you prefer bungee jumping.

3. Use a comma after an introductory clause (starting with a conjunction such as "although," "if" or "until":
> When the skies clear, I plan to go for a walk.

4. Use a comma after an introductory phrase if it contains three or more words:
> Under the waving flag, I met a stranger.

5. Use a comma to set off parenthetical words, phrases, and clauses that are placed in the middle of a sentence:
> The artist, who never said a word, drew a boat.

6. Use a comma to set off the name of the person or persons spoken to:
> Listen to me, Fred.

7. Use a comma between two adjectives:
> It was a large, red truck.

8. Use a comma to set off interjections and other expressions that interrupt the flow of the sentence:
> Aha, this must be the place.

Comma splice: Two sentences awkwardly joined by a comma, for example:
> I went to the store, my friend met me there.

One solution is to substitute a period for the comma and capitalize the first word in the second sentence:
> I went to the store. My friend met me there.

Contraction: A word formed by leaving out letters or by merging two words. Examples include "can't," "don't," "isn't," "shouldn't," and "won't." When spelling a contraction, be sure to put the apostrophe only where one or more letters have been omitted.

Editing Guide

Dangling participle: A descriptive phrase with no subject to describe, often creating a silly sentence:

    Walking across the street, the house looked strange.

To avoid the problem, add a subject:

    Walking across the street, I saw a strange house.

Dash: A punctuation mark — used to separate words.
1. Use a dash to set off parenthetical words from the rest of the sentence:

    At the bakery—the one in the mall—I bought a cake.
2. Instead of a colon, you can use a dash before a list:

    We visited three cities—Miami, Memphis, and Tulsa.

Exclamation point: A punctuation mark ! used to show emotion. Place an exclamation point at the end of a sentence or quotation:

    "This won't do!" shouted the giant.

Hyphen: A punctuation mark - used in spelling.
1. Use a hyphen to break a word at the end of a line if the word doesn't fit; the hyphen should go only between syllables and never within a syllable:

    On our vacation our family went to the sea-shore.
2. Use a hyphen to join two words to create a new (hyphenated) word:

    I like to eat Martian-American food.

Lower-case letters: The letters a, b, c, and d rather than capital letters A, B, C, and D.

Paragraph: A group of sentences that works as a unit. A paragraph is set off by indenting the first line (moving it a few spaces to the right) or by blank lines.

Parallelism: Using the same grammatical form in a list, for example, all verbs:

    I ride, run, and jump.

Editing Guide

Parentheses: Punctuation marks ( ) that set apart a word or phrase from the rest of a sentence:

The Eiffel Tower is 984 feet (300 meters) high.

Passive voice: A form of the sentence in which the subject receives the action:

I was scared by the storm.

For more dramatic and more concise writing, try turning the passive voice into the active voice:

The storm scared me.

Period: A punctuation mark . used at the end of a sentence and to form abbreviations.

Possessive: The form of a noun or pronoun that shows ownership. With most nouns, the possessive singular is formed by adding 's:

The cat's dish is full.

The possessive plural noun is formed by adding ' to the plural noun:

The dogs' barking kept me away.

If the plural does not end in s, the possessive is formed by adding 's:

The men's department is on the second floor.

Never use an apostrophe with possessive pronouns (hers, his, its, theirs, yours, ours):

The book is hers.

Pronoun: A word that replaces a noun.

Personal pronouns: I, me, you, he, she, it, we, us, our, they, them.

Possessive pronouns: my, mine, your, yours, his, her, its, our, ours, their, theirs.

Relative pronouns: who, whom, that, which.

1. Use pronouns to avoid repeating the noun. Instead of:

I like to watch movies. Movies can be exciting.

Try:

I like to watch movies. They can be exciting.

2. Make it clear which word the pronoun replaces. Otherwise, readers can be confused.

Editing Guide

Proper noun: The name of a particular person, place, or thing, the opposite of a common noun. Proper nouns are almost always capitalized, for example:
    Joan of Arc, Chicago, the Titanic

Quotation marks: A form of punctuation " " used to identify words spoken by a character or written by someone other than the author.
1. Use quotation marks to set off dialogue:
    Then the giant screamed, "Fe, fi, fo, fum!"
2. Place quotation marks around words being discussed:
    I have trouble spelling "pneumonia."

Redundant: A repetitious word or phrase. For example, in the phrase "the month of May," "month" is redundant because May, by definition, is a month.

Run-on sentence: A group of words punctuated as a sentence but consisting of two sentences that should stand alone. Run-on sentences can be confusing:
    I went to the bank unfortunately it was closed.
To correct this error, insert the missing punctuation and capitalize the first word in the second sentence:
    I went to the bank. Unfortunately, it was closed.

Semicolon: A punctuation mark ; used in place of a period to show that two ideas are closely related:
    That student is a hero; she rang the fire alarm.

Sentence fragment: A group of words punctuated as a sentence but lacking either a subject or a verb or both:
    Reading a book. That's fun.
Because sentence fragments can confuse readers, editors usually turn them into complete sentences:
    Reading a book can be fun.
Sentence fragments are acceptable in dialogue because people often talk in sentence fragments:
    "Where are you going?" I asked my friend.
    "To the store."

Editing Guide

Spelling error: A word written incorrectly ("frend" for "friend") or a word confused with another word, for example, "its" and "it's." The following tips may help:
1. Read your writing slowly or aloud.
2. Watch out for sound-alike words: "your" and "you're."
3. Watch out for look-alike words: "though" and "through."
4. Don't blend two words that should be spelled separately: "high school."
5. Look up every word you're not sure of.

Synonyms: Two words with similar meanings, for example, "small" and "tiny." Synonyms are helpful when revising sentences with annoying word repetitions:

The right way to go is to turn right at the corner.
The correct way to go is to turn right at the corner.

Tense: The time when an action occurs. Three often-used tenses are:

Present tense: I laugh now.
Past tense: I laughed then.
Future tense: I will laugh tomorrow.

Don't randomly switch tenses. It's usually best to use one tense throughout a piece of writing.

Underlining: A form of punctuation _____ used to highlight words.
1. Underline book titles:
    The Wizard of Oz
If you have a computer, you might use italic letters:
    The Wizard of Oz
2. Underline words discussed as words:
    Do you know the plural of <u>mongoose</u>?
The other choice is to put the words in quotation marks.

Wordiness: Using extra words. Writers usually try to get rid of every word that isn't needed. For example, "My sister is a girl who plays the piano" is wordier than "My sister plays the piano."

EDITING MARKS

Editors use the following marks to make changes on a manuscript.

Mark	**Meaning of the Mark**
atlete	Insert a letter, a word, or a punctuation mark.
It's (very) cold.	Delete a letter, word, or words.
It's ~~easy~~. (quick)	Delete the crossed out material and replace it with the material above.
He (widely) smiles.	Move the enclosed material to where the arrow points.
I see⊙	Insert a period or change the punctuation to a period.
¶ The dog barked.	Start a new paragraph here.
⌐ The dog barked.	Start a new paragraph here. (alternate mark)
high#school	Insert a space.
un ( ) til	Move together.
omaha	Capitalize this letter.
I can /ki.	Make this letter lower case.
olny	Reverse the order of letters or words.

Using Editing Marks

Here are three versions of the same short story. The first draft contains many errors. The second draft has been corrected using editing marks. The third draft has been reprinted based on the corrections in the second draft.

First Draft

When People first saw a camel they shreeked with fear & ran, after they realizzed it was harm less they decided then that the camel couldbe put it to work. The moral are dont fear teh unknown

Edited Draft

When People first saw a camel they shreeked with fear & ran, after they realizzed it was harm less they decided then that the camel couldbe put it to work. The moral are dont fear teh unknown

Final Draft

When people first saw a camel, they shrieked with fear and ran. After they realized that it was harmless, they then decided that the camel could be put to work.

The moral is: Don't fear the unknown.

EDITING NOTES

To the teacher:

Students can sharpen their editing skills while giving feedback to their classmates. Instead of making changes on a partner's manuscript, each editor places notes in the margins, alerting the writer of problems. This allows the writer to take responsibility for making the changes. (If you prefer, you can ask the student editors to draw a line to the problem.)

Before students actually comment on each other's papers, let them practice on a sample manuscript, such as the one below. You'll find an unmarked, reproducible version of this material on the next page. After students work on it, have a class discussion of their notes.

1   Fun City hotel   *capitalization*

2   Are you tired and ready for fun. If the answer   *punctuation*

3   is yes, then come spend time at the the Fun City   *repeated word*

4   hotel on Shell Beach. You can get hear by car, train,   *spelling (homonym)*

5   boat or plane. Then the fun begins. Our top four

6   activities is swiming, boating, waterskiing,   *fact error / agreement (verb)*

7   snorkeling and to fish. As for food, our chefs come

8   from england, germany, and italy. You can eat in   *capitalization*

9   our beautifully dining hall overlooking the oceans,   *wrong form of word*

10   or you can dine on the outdoor patio?   *wrong form / punctuation*

11   The price is always fair at Fun City. For one   *punctuation*

12   low payment you get meals, and beach equipment.

86

Editing Notes

Imagine that you work in an advertising company. A writer has just finished an ad for a newspaper. Your job is to make notes in the margin, pointing out mistakes that the writer should deal with. Look for spelling errors, missing words, repeated words, missing paragraph breaks, and other problems.

Don't correct the mistakes yourself. The writer will do that using the notes that you put in the margins.

1   Fun City hotel

2   Are you tired and ready for fun. If the answer

3   is yes, then come spend time at the the Fun City

4   hotel on Shell Beach. You can get hear by car, train,

5   boat or plane. Then the fun begins. Our top four

6   activities is swiming, boating, waterskiing,

7   snorkeling and to fish. As for food, our chefs come

8   from england, germany, and italy. You can eat in

9   our beautifuly dining hall overlooking the oceans,

10   or you can dine on the outdoor patio?

11   The price is always fair at Fun City. For one

12   low payment you get meals, and beach equipment.

HOMONYM RIDDLES

Which homonym fits in which blank?

1. Are we _____ to read _____ in the library? (aloud, allowed)

2. My _____ Jennie watched a little red _____ climb the wall. (aunt, ant)

3. All _____ of us _____ the cake, and it tasted good. (ate, eight)

4. To cool the soup, I _____ so hard my face turned _____. (blew, blue)

5. If you don't use your bike's _____, you can _____ a leg. (brake, break)

6. Please _____ the door to your _____ closet. (close, clothes)

7. Oh, _____, the _____ are eating all my flowers. (dear, deer)

8. It's not _____ that the bus company is raising its _____. (fair, fare)

9. If you want to _____ the music, stand right _____. (hear, here)

10. I _____ the pounding hoofbeats of a _____ of cattle. (heard, herd)

11. I tried to _____ my sore _____ by not walking on it. (heal, heel)

12. You don't have to be a _____ to deliver the _____. (mail, male)

13. After carrying the _____ of water, Jack and Jill were _____. (pail, pale)

14. I bought a _____ for my boat and saved money because it was on _____. (sale, sail)

15. I gave valentines _____ _____ of my friends (to, two)

PRONOUN ANTECEDENTS

At the heart of the correct pronoun is the concept of the antecedent. The antecedent is the word that the pronoun replaces (refers to). In the sentence "The dog lost its collar" the antecedent of "its" is "dog." Antecedent means "going before," but the antecedent can follow the pronoun, for example, "We, the people..."

There's a simple way to make students aware of the relationship between the antecedent and its pronoun.

1. On the board, write a sentence containing a noun and a pronoun. Underline the pronoun, or ask students to do it.
   Love your enemies, for <u>they</u> tell you your faults.
2. Ask students to draw an arrow from the pronoun to its antecedent.
   Love your enemies, for (they) tell you your faults.
3. On the board or in a handout, repeat this activity with sentences containing a variety of pronouns:

   Happy is the house <u>that</u> shelters a friend.

   Intelligence is quickness in seeing things as <u>they</u> are.

   Beware of the man <u>who</u> won't be bothered with details.

Note: Pronouns may refer to antecedents outside the writing:

   <u>You</u> [the reader] are what you do.

4. Because pronouns often refer to a noun in a previous sentence, sometimes present two sentences:

   We should not only use the brains we have. We should use <u>those</u> we can borrow.

5. After students master the idea of antecedent, they will be ready to correct sentences in which the pronoun doesn't agree with the noun, or in which the pronoun doesn't even have a clear antecedent.

SPELLING DEMONS

absence
accept
accidentally
accommodate
across
address
affect
again
all right
a lot
already
among
amount
angle
answer
appear
Arctic
argument
article
ask
athletics
author

balloon
beautiful
because
beginning
believe
burglar
business
busy

calendar
capital
capitol
captain
careful
character

choose
chief
cigarette
clothes
coarse
college
color
coming
committee
completely
conscience
conscious
control
council
counsel
counterfeit
county
country
course
cruelly

decide
defense
definite
democracy
description
desert
dessert
develop
different
disappear
disappoint
disastrous
discipline
doctor
dye
dying

eighth
embarrass
emperor
English
enormous
exaggerate
excellent
except
excitement
exercise
existence
experience
experiment
explanation
extraordinary
extravagant
extremely

Fahrenheit
familiar
family
February
finally
foreigner
fortunately
forty
fourteen
fourth
friend
fulfil
furniture

government
governor
grammar
guarantee
guard
guess

handkerchief
heaven
height
heir
hero, heroes
high school
history
humor
humorous
hungrily
hygiene

identical
illegible
immediately
in between
independence
in fact
inoculate
in spite of
intelligence
interesting
its (possessive)
it's ("it is")

jealous
judgment

knew
know
knowledge

laboratory
laid (never
  "layed")
language
lead (I lead)
led (I have led)

Spelling Demons

library
license
lightning
loneliness
loose
lose

marriage
mathematics
meant
medicine
medieval
Mediterranean
messenger
miniature
minute
misspell
motor
mystery

naturally
necessary
neighbor
ninth
no one
noticeable
nuisance

occasionally
occurrence
old-fashioned
omission
opinion
opportunity
ordinarily

paid
parallel

passed
past
perhaps
permanent
permission
personal
physician
piece
pigeon
playwright
pleasant
poison
possession
precede
prejudice
preparation
primitive
principal (chief)
principle (rule)
privilege
prize
probably
proceed
pronunciation
propeller
pursue

quietly

really
receipt
receive
recommend
referee
refrigerator
religious
repetition
reservoir

restaurant
rhyme
rhythm
ridiculous

safety
satellite
scenery
schedule
science
scissors
secretary
seize
sense
sentence
separate
sergeant
sheriff
silhouette
similar
sincerely
skillful
soldier
souvenir
speech
studying
succeed
successfully
summarize
surely
surprise

temperature
temporary
their (possessive)
therefore
they're ("they
    are")

though
threw (the ball)
through (a door)
tobacco
toboggan
together
tomorrow
tongue
too
tragedy
tried
truly
Tuesday
twelfth
tying

until
usually

vacuum
valleys
valuable
vegetable
vehicle
veterinary
villain

weather
Wednesday
weird
whether
who's ("who is")
whose
    (possessive)
woman
writing

SPELLING TRICKS

Some tricky-to-spell words contain silent letters or letter sequences that violate the usual spelling pattern. Others are confusing because they are homonyms. If repeated drill doesn't help, making up a memory trick (a mnemonic) can solve the problem. A spelling mnemonic links an easy-to-spell word with a tricky word. You can create your own based on the following models.

Word-within-a-word Trick
Look for an easy-to-spell word contained in the difficult word. Then relate the two words in a sentence:
> I want a piece of pie.
> Don't be late for your chocolate.
> That pigeon made a pig of itself.
> I carried a cross across the street.

Definition Trick
Find a simple word that helps define the tricky word and that also has a shared letter pattern:
> An altar is a kind of table.
> When you sop up water with a blotter, that's absorption.

Synonym Trick
Find an easy-to-spell synonym that contains a letter pattern related to the tricky word:
> An inoculation is an injection.
> Adjust means adapt.

Story-sentence Trick
List several words that pose a similar problem and combine them in an easy-to-remember "story" sentence:
> They held out their palms for alms while singing psalms.
> Our heroes used tomatoes and potatoes in their torpedoes.

Word-family Trick
Find a related word whose pronunciation highlights a silent-letter problem in the tricky word:
> A muscular person has muscles.

WORDS TO WATCH

accept, except: "Accept" means "take what is given"; "except" means "not counting."

> I can't accept your invitation if you invite everyone except my sister.

actually: This word usually adds little to a sentence.

all right: This is the preferred spelling.

among, between: "Among" refers to three or more; "between" refers to two.

> The pizza was shared among the five of us.
> The prize was divided between Allison and Ralph.

amount, number: Measure an amount; count a number,

> The bin contains a large amount of flour.
> A number of people visited Bea in the hospital.

anecdote, antidote: "Anecdote" is a story; "antidote" is a cure.

> An amusing anecdote is an antidote to boredom.

anyway: This word should never end with an s.

beside/besides: "Beside" means "next to"; "besides" means "also."

> I'll sit beside you because you're my friend. Besides, there's no other place to sit.

breath, breathe: "Breath" is a quantity of air; to "breathe" is to "inhale and exhale."

> Take a big breath. Breathe slowly.

bring, take: "Bring" means "move toward the speaker"; "take" means "move away."

> Please bring me that photo so that I can look at it.
> Please take this photo to the store for framing.

compare, contrast: "Compare" means "to show how two things are alike and different"; contrast means "to show how two things are different."

Words to Watch

emigrate, immigrate: "Emigrate" means "to move from a country"; "immigrate" means "to move into a country."

fact, opinion: "Fact" is "an observation"; "opinion" is "a belief."

> It's a fact that water freezes at 0 degrees Celsius.
> It's an opinion that basketball is more fun than soccer.

I'm going to lie down.

farther, further: "Farther" relates to distance; "further" relates to degree.

> We ran farther than they did.
> My art project is further along than yours.

fewer, less: "Fewer" relates to counting; "less" relates to measure.

> We saw fewer squirrels this year than last year.
> There is less water in the lake this year than last year.

flammable, inflammable: Both words mean "burnable."

funny: Don't label a story "funny." Let your audience decide.

human, humane: "Human" refers to people who think; "humane" means "kind."

imply, infer: "Imply" means "suggest." "Infer" means "understand."

I'm going to lay an egg.

interesting: Instead of saying that you have an interesting story, tell the story and let others decide if it's interesting.

irregardless: The correct word is "regardless."

its, it's: "Its" is a possessive pronoun; "it's" is a contraction.

kind of: Avoid this in sentences like "He's kind of busy."

lay, lie: "Lay" means "to put (something) down"; "lie" means "to recline."

> The hen lays an egg. I lie down after eating.

Words to Watch

leave, let: "Leave" means "go away"; "let" means "allow."
  Let me see you before I leave for Paris.

literally: Because "literally" means "in fact," don't use it to describe impossible situations, for example, "the room literally exploded with laughter."

loose, lose: "Loose" means "free"; "lose" means "misplace."

nice: Avoid this overused word.

personal, personnel: "Personal" means "private"; "personnel" means "workers."
  This matter is too personal to talk about.
  I'd like to interview some of your company's personnel.

precede, proceed: "Precede" means "to go before"; "proceed" means "to begin."
  My grandmother preceded me into the auditorium.
  Let's proceed with the play.

really: Avoid this overused word.

role, roll: "Role" means "a part in a play or in an organization"; "roll" means "a list."
  I got the lead role in the play.
  My teacher called the roll.

sort of: Avoid this phrase in sentences such as "I was sort of happy."

very: Avoid this overused word.

BIBLIOGRAPHY

The following books, which were consulted during the writing of *Ten-Minute Editing Skill Builders*, may prove useful for developing additional editing practices for your classroom.

The Careful Writer: A Modern Guide to English Usage by Theodore Bernstein (Atheneum, 1983). This highly readable reference provides background information on all sorts of wording problems, from accidental puns to deciding whether to use "Ye" (as in "Ye Old Coach House").

The Concise Columbia Encyclopedia (Avon, 1983). Including factual sentences in the daily edit can add to your students' general knowledge.

Demonic Mnemonics by Murray Suid (Fearon, 1981). Here's a source of hundreds of ready-to-use spelling tricks.

Edit Yourself: A Manual for Everyone Who Works with Words by Bruce Ross-Larson (Norton, 1982). The book contains scores of editing tips and phrases for use in editing exercises.

The Elements of Grammar by Margaret Shertzer (Macmillan, 1986). If you want to survey every aspect of grammar in a few pages, this book is the answer.

The Elements of Style by William Strunk, Jr., and E.B. White (Macmillan, 1979). This is the most popular book about clear writing.

Teacher's Quotation Book: Little Lessons on Learning, collected by Wanda Lincoln and Murray Suid (Dale Seymour, 1986). Quotation books are useful for introducing students to great writers and thinkers while giving practice in the art of editing.

There's No Zoo in Zoology and Other Beastly Mispronunciations by Charles Elster (Macmillan, 1988). Because mispronunciation contributes to spelling woes, this collection of frequently garbled words is a rich source of words for the daily edit.